Shakespeare Redacted

Shakespeare Redacted

Shakespeare edited by the blasphemous rogue
Stephen Cramer

SHANTI ARTS PUBLISHING
BRUNSWICK, MAINE

Shakespeare Redacted

Copyright © 2024 Stephen Cramer

All Rights Reserved
No part of this document may be reproduced or transmitted in any form or by any means without prior written permission of the publisher, except where permitted by law.

Published by Shanti Arts Publishing

Designed by Shanti Arts Designs

Cover image: The portrait of William Shakespeare was engraved by Martin Droeshout and served as the frontispiece for the title page of the First Folio collection of Shakespeare's plays, published in 1623. Wikimedia Commons. Public domain.

Shanti Arts LLC
193 Hillside Road
Brunswick, Maine 04011
shantiarts.com

Printed in the United States of America

ISBN: 978-1-962082-47-1 (softcover)

Library of Congress Control Number (LCCN): 2024951357

•

The author wishes to acknowledge the English Department at The University of Vermont for sponsoring a research trip to London and the Globe Theater.

For Joanna, whose demanding work schedule one summer all but dictated that I fill in the gaps of my Shakespeare.

"When you depart from me,
sorrow abides and happiness takes his leave."

—*Much Ado About Nothing*

Also by Stephen Cramer

Shiva's Drum

Tongue & Groove

From the Hip

A Little Thyme & A Pinch of Rhyme

Bone Music

A Jar of Moon Air: Selected Poems of Jaime Sabines
(translated with Alejandro Merizalde)

Turn It Up! Music in Poetry from Jazz to Hip-Hop
(editor)

The Hot Sauce Madness Love Burn Suite:
814 Couplets About Hot Sauce

The Disintegration Loops

City Full of Fireworks and Blues

Shakespeare Unscene: Dialogues that Madeth Not the Final Cut

Contents

Introduction — 13

Section One—Enter

Twelfth Night, or What You Will / Music Be So Sweet — 16
The Famous History of the Life of King Henry the Eighth /
    I Come Out of Hope — 18
Life and Death of Richard the Third / A Smile Says — 20
The Merry Wives of Windsor / You Do Amaze — 22
A Midsummer Night's Dream / Mend — 24
The Second Part of Henry the Sixth, with the Death
    of the Good Duke Humphrey / Your Presence — 26
Much Ado about Nothing / The World Is Giddy — 28
The Taming of the Shrew / Place Your Hand — 30
The Tragedy of Julius Caesar / What Art Thou? — 32
The Winter's Tale / Believe Me — 34
The Tragedy of Antony and Cleopatra / It Be Love — 36
The Second Part of King Henry the Sixth / More Such Days — 38
The Tragedy of Othello / Dream — 40
The Tragedy of Othello / You Are Hell — 42
Richard the Second / I Wander through Thy Light — 44
The Tragedy of King Lear / O, O, O, O — 46
Much Ado about Nothing / In Letters — 48
The Tragedy of Julius Caesar / His Bones — 50
Timon of Athens / Memory — 52
The Life and Death of King John / Come Home — 54
The Two Gentlemen of Verona / My Valentine — 56
The Tragedy of Cymbeline / The Bent Heart — 58
The Life of Henry the Fifth / The Garden — 60
The First Part of Henry the Sixth / Youth — 62
The First Part of Henry the Fourth / Another Day — 64

The First Part of Henry the Fourth / Shaken 66
Love's Labour's Lost / Time 68
The Tragedy of Macbeth / The Snares of Life 70
The Famous History of the Life of King Henry the Eighth /
    Such Art 72
The Tragedy of King John / Silence 74
The Merchant of Venice / Sadness 76
A Comedy of Errors / A Question 78
The Tragedy of Hamlet, Prince of Denmark / Wild Like Music ... 80
The Lamentable Tragedy of Titus Andronicus / Loving Words ... 82
The First Part of Henry the Sixth / Wider 84
The Taming of the Shrew / Remedy 86
The Most Excellent and Lamentable Tragedy of Romeo and Juliet /
    Both Like 88

Section Two—Exeunt

The Tempest / Bestir 92
The Tragedy of King Lear / Curiosity 94
The Tragedy of King Richard the Second / The Sound Ancient ... 96
The Comedy of Errors / Proceed 98
The Tragedy of Troilus and Cressida / Expectation 100
King Henry the Sixth, Part Three / Our Lasting Joy 102
A Midsummer Night's Dream / Spirit of Mirth 104
Measure for Measure / Speech 106
The Life of Timon of Athens / Good Day, Pain 108
Troilus and Cressida / Seek 110
The Two Gentlemen of Verona / We Will Dare 112
The Tragedy of Cymbeline / Our Crooked Temple 114
The Play of Pericles, Prince of Tyre / Glorious 116
The Tragedy of Romeo and Juliet / This Morning 118
All's Well that Ends Well / Take Heart 120
Measure for Measure / Thanks 122
As You Like It / My Kind Offer 124

The Second Part of King Henry the Fourth, the Induction /
   Blunt Monster 126
The Tragedy of Macbeth / When 128
The Tragedy of Coriolanus / Before We Speak 130
The Winter's Tale / In Vain 132
Twelfth Night / I Rain 134
The Tragedy of Titus Andronicus / Her 136
The Merchant of Venice / Keep Safe 138
Antony and Cleopatra / Infinite Ways 140
The Tragedy of Richard the Third / The Clouds 142
The Tragedy of Coriolanus / The Best of It 144
All's Well That Ends Well / Hope 146
As You Like It / This Nothing 148
The Tragedy of Hamlet, Prince of Denmark / I Hear Them 150
King Henry the Fourth / Pray 152
The Merry Wives of Windsor / O Page 154
The Life of Henry the Fifth / Within 156
The Third Part of Henry the Sixth, with the Death of the Duke
   of York / What I Did 158
Love's Labour's Lost / Milk 160
The Tempest / Release Me 162
Play of Pericles, Prince of Tyre / Evermore Joy 164

About the Author 167

Introduction

It feels both odd and exhilarating to have created a book without having written a single word. Truly, none of the words herein are my own. In these blackout poems, I have taken the first and last pages of each of Shakespeare's thirty-eight* plays and simply crossed out the majority of words in order to come up with my own "poems."

It makes me think of the two ways that one can create sculpture. One can, like Rodin, pile clay on top of clay to construct an image. Or one can, like Michelangelo, take a piece of marble and chisel away at it to discover the form within. This project, at least when envisioned as a collaboration, has felt like a combination of both of these approaches. Shakespeare has provided the materials, and I have chiseled away at them to find a new form within. Now, I am loathe to have my name anywhere in the vicinity of Shakespeare, Michelangelo, or Rodin; this is simply a description of process.

It honestly feels more than a bit subversive to deface the most revered of texts, but the possibility of collaborating with the greatest author of all time was just too great an opportunity to pass up. In order to fully acknowledge all of my collaborators, let me add that these pages have been lifted from *The Yale Shakespeare* series, a forty-volume set, originally published between the years 1918 and 1928.

In any case, all apologies and gratitude to the Bard.

---

*Well, thirty-seven actually. The Yale set omits *The Two Noble Kinsmen*, which wasn't accepted into the cannon until years later.

Section One
Enter

Twelfth Night, or What You Will

[Act 1, Scene 1]

DUKE If music be the food of love, play on!
Give me excess of it, that, surfeiting,
The appetite may sicken and so die.
That strain again! it had a dying fall;
O, it came o'er my ear like the sweet sound,
That breathes upon a bank of violets,
Stealing and giving odor. Enough, no more;
'Tis not so sweet now as it was before.
O spirit of love! how quick and fresh art thou,
That, notwithstanding thy capacity,
Receiveth as the sea. Nought enters there,
Of what validity and pitch soe'er,
But falls into abatement and low price,
Even in a minute. So full of shapes is fancy
That it alone is high fantastical.
CURIO Will you go hunt, my lord?

Music Be So Sweet

music be

so

sweet

so sweet

and fresh

That it

enters

and

shapes

you

THE FAMOUS HISTORY OF THE LIFE OF KING HENRY THE EIGHTH

[Prologue]

I come no more to make you laugh: things now,
That bear a weighty and a serious brow,
Sad, high, and working, full of state and woe,
Such noble scenes as draw the eye to flow,
We now present. Those that can pity here
May, if they think it well, let fall a tear;
The subject will deserve it. Such as give
Their money out of hope they may believe,
May here find truth too. Those that come to see
Only a show or two, and so agree
The play may pass, if they be still and willing,
I'll undertake may see away their shilling
Richly in two short hours. Only they
That come to hear a merry bawdy play,
A noise of targets, or to see a fellow
In a long motley coat guarded with yellow,
Will be deceiv'd; for, gentle hearers, know,
To rank our chosen truth with such a show
As fool and fight is, beside forfeiting
Our own brains, and the opinion that we bring,
To make that only true we now intend,
Will leave us never an understanding friend.
Therefore, for goodness' sake, and as you are known
The first and happiest hearers of the town,

I Come Out of Hope

I come

out of hope

that

merry

noise

Will leave us never

Life and Death of Richard the Third

[End of Act 5]

Proclaim a pardon to the soldiers fled
That in submission will return to us;
And then, as we have ta'en the sacrament,
We will unite the white rose and the red:
Smile heaven upon this fair conjunction,
That long have frown'd upon their enmity!
What traitor hears me, and says not amen?
England hath long been mad, and scarr'd herself;
The brother blindly shed the brother's blood,
The father rashly slaughter'd his own son,
The son, compell'd, been butcher to the sire:
All this divided York and Lancaster,
Divided in their dire division,
O, now let Richmond and Elizabeth,
The true succeeders of each royal house,
By God's fair ordinance conjoin together;
And let their heirs—God, if thy will be so,—
Enrich the time to come with smooth-fac'd peace,
With smiling plenty and fair prosperous days!
Abate the edge of traitors, gracious Lord,
That would reduce these bloody days again,
And make poor England weep in streams of blood!
Let them not live to taste this land's increase,
That would with treason wound this fair land's peace!
Now civil wounds are stopp'd, peace lives again:
That she may long live here, God say amen!

A Smile Says

a
Smile
says
she
is
compell'd to
be
together
And will
smooth
the edge of
these
wound s

The Merry Wives of Windsor

[End of Act 5]

PAGE Now, mistress, how chance you went not with Master Slender?
MRS. PAGE Why went you not with Master Doctor, maid?
FENT You do amaze her: hear the truth of it.
You would have married her most shamefully,
Where there was no proportion held in love.
The truth is, she and I, long since contracted,
Are now so sure that nothing can dissolve us.
The offence is holy that she hath committed,
And this deceit loses the name of craft,
Of disobedience, or unduteous title,
Since therein she doth evitate and shun
A thousand irreligious cursed hours,
Which forced marriage would have brought upon her.
FORD Stand not amazed; here is no remedy:
In love the heavens themselves do guide the state:
Money buys lands, and wives are sold by fate.
FAL I am glad, though you have ta'en a special stand to
strike at me, that your arrow hath glanced.
PAGE Well, what remedy?—Fenton, heaven give thee joy!
What cannot be eschew'd must be embrac'd.
FAL When night-dogs run, all sorts of deer are chas'd.
MRS. PAGE Well, I will muse no further. Master Fenton,
Heaven give you many, many merry days!
Good husband, let us every one go home,
And laugh this sport o'er by a country fire;
Sir John and all.
FORD Let it be so. Sir John,
To Master Brook you yet shall hold your word;
For he tonight shall lie with Mistress Ford.

You Do Amaze

Now, mistress,

You do amaze

A thousand

heavens

When night

let's
this sport
be so.

A Midsummer Night's Dream

[End of Act 5]

Think but this, and all is mended,
That you have but slumber'd here
While these visions did appear.
And this weak and idle theme,
No more yielding but a dream,
Gentles, do not reprehend:
if you pardon, we will mend.
And, as I'm an honest Puck,
If we have unearned luck
Now to 'scape the serpent's tongue,
We will make amends ere long;
Else the Puck a liar call:
So, good night unto you all.
Give me your hands, if we be friends,
And Robin shall restore amends.

Mend

this

weak and idle
dream
will mend

the tongue,
will mend
the
night
Give me your hands
to mend

The Second Part of Henry the Sixth, with the Death of the Good Duke Humphrey

[Act 1, Scene 1]

SUF   As by your high imperial majesty
I had in charge at my depart for France,
As procurator to your excellence,
To marry Princess Margaret for your Grace;
So, in the famous ancient city, Tours,
In presence of the Kings of France and Sicil,
The Dukes of Orleans, Calaber, Britaine and Alencon,
Seven earls, twelve barons, and twenty reverend bishops,
I have perform'd my task and was espoused:
And humbly now upon my bended knee,
In sight of England and her lordly peers,
Deliver up my title in the queen
To your most gracious hands, that are the substance
Of that great shadow I did represent;
The happiest gift that ever marquess gave,
The fairest queen that ever king receiv'd.

Your Presence

your

presence

was

a

great shadow
The happiest gift that
ever i receiv'd.

MUCH ADO ABOUT NOTHING

[End of Act 5]

brief, since I do purpose to marry, I will think nothing to any purpose that the world can say against it; and therefore never flout at me for what I have said against it, for man is a giddy thing, and this is my conclusion. For thy part, Claudio, I did think to have beaten thee; but, in that thou art like to be my kinsman, live unbruised, and love my cousin.
CLAUD I had well hoped thou wouldst have denied Beatrice, that I might have cudgelled thee out of thy single life, to make thee a double-dealer; which, out of question, thou wilt be, if my cousin do not look exceedingly narrowly to thee.
BENE Come, come, we are friends. Let's have a dance ere we are married, that we may lighten our own hearts and our wives' heels.
LEON We'll have dancing afterward.
BENE First, of my word: therefore play, Music! Prince, thou art sad; get thee a wife, get thee a wife: there is no staff more reverend than one tipped with horn.

[Enter Messenger]

MES My lord, your brother John is ta'en in flight,
And brought with armed men back to Messina.
BEN Think not on him till to-morrow: I'll devise thee brave punishments for him. Strikeup, pipers.

[Dance]

The World Is Giddy

The Taming of the Shrew

[End of Act 5]

Our strength as weak, our weakness past compare,
That seeming to be most which we indeed least are.
Then vail your stomachs, for it is no boot,
And place your hands below your husband's foot:
In token of which duty, if he please,
My hand is ready; may it do him ease.
PETRUCHIO   Why, there's a wench! Come on, and kiss me, Kate.
LUCENTIO   Well, go thy ways, old lad, for thou shalt ha't.
VINCENTIO   'Tis a good hearing when children are toward.
LUCENTIO   But a harsh hearing when women are froward.
PETRUCHIO   Come, Kate, we'll to bed.
We three are married, but you two are sped.
'Twas I won the wager, [To LUCENTIO] though you hit the white;
And, being a winner, God give you good night!

[Exit Petruchio, with Katherina]

HORTENSIO   Now, go thy ways; thou hast tam'd a curst shrow.
LUCENTIO   'Tis a wonder, by your leave, she will be tam'd so.

Place Your Hand

THE TRAGEDY OF JULIUS CAESAR

[Act 1, Scene 1]

FLAV... Hence! home, you idle creatures, get you home:
Is this a holiday? What! know you not,
Being mechanical, you ought not walk
Upon a labouring day without the sign
Of your profession? Speak, what trade art thou?
CAR Why, sir, a carpenter.
MAR Where is thy leather apron, and thy rule?
What dost thou with thy best apparel on?
You, sir, what trade are you?
COB Truly, sir, in respect of a fine workman, I am but, as you would say, a cobbler.
MAR But what trade art thou? Answer me directly.
COB A trade, sir, that, I hope, I may use with a safe conscience; which is, indeed, sir, a mender of bad soles.
MAR What trade, thou knave? thou naughty knave, what trade?

WHAT ART THOU?

The Winter's Tale

[Act 1, Scene 1]

ARCH If you shall chance, Camillo, to visit Bohemia, on the like occasion whereon my services are now on foot, you shall see, as I have said, great difference betwixt our Bohemia and your Sicilia.
CAM I think, this coming summer, the King of Sicilia means to pay Bohemia the visitation which he justly owes him.
ARCH Wherein our entertainment shall shame us we will be justified in our loves; for indeed—
CAM Beseech you,—
ARCH Verily, I speak it in the freedom of my knowledge: we cannot with such magnificence—in so rare—I know not what to say. We will give you sleepy drinks, that your senses, unintelligent of our insufficiency, may, though they cannot praise us, as little accuse us.
CAM You pay a great deal too dear for what's given freely.
ARCH Believe me, I speak as my understanding instructs me, and as mine honesty puts it to utterance.

Believe Me

you shall

this coming summer

drink

a great deal
Believe me

The Tragedy of Antony and Cleopatra

[Act 1, Scene 1]

PHILO Nay, but this dotage of our general's
O'erflows the measure: those his goodly eyes,
That o'er the files and musters of the war
Have glow'd like plated Mars, now bend, now turn
The office and devotion of their view
Upon a tawny front: his captain's heart,
Which in the scuffles of great fights hath burst
The buckles on his breast, reneges all temper,
And is become the bellows and the fan
To cool a gypsy's lust.

[Enter Antony, Cleopatra, her Ladies,
the train, with Eunuchs fanning her]

Look! where they come:
Take but good note, and you shall see in him.
The triple pillar of the world transform'd
Into a strumpet's fool. Behold and see.
CLEOPATRA If it be love indeed, tell me how much.

It Be Love

his   eyes

Have glow'd

his   heart
            hath burst

Look!   they come:

              Behold
         it be love

The Second Part of King Henry the Sixth

[End of Act 5]

But still, where danger was, still there I met him;
And like rich hangings in a homely house,
So was his will in his old feeble body.
But, noble as he is, look where he comes.

[Enter Salisbury]

SAL   Now, by my sword, well hast thou fought to-day;
By the mass, so did we all. I thank you, Richard:
God knows how long it is I have to live;
And it hath pleased him that three times to-day
You have defended me from imminent death.
Well, lords, we have not got that which we have:
'Tis not enough our foes are this time fled,
Being opposites of such repairing nature.
YORK   I know our safety is to follow them;
For, as I hear, the king is fled to London,
To call a present court of parliament:
Let us pursue him ere the writs go forth:—
What says Lord Warwick? shall we after them?
War. After them! nay, before them, if we can.
Now, by my faith, lords, 'twas a glorious day:
Saint Albans battle, won by famous York,
Shall be eterniz'd in all age to come.
Sound, drums and trumpets, and to London all:
And more such days as these to us befall!

More Such Days

danger

comes.

we all
know how

imminent death

is

Let us pursue
What
we can.
'twas a glorious day:

And more such days as these to us befall!

The Tragedy of Othello

[Act 1, Scene 1]

ROD Tush! never tell me! I take it much unkindly
That thou, Iago, who hast had my purse
As if the strings were thine, shouldst know of this.
IAGO 'Sblood, but you will not hear me!
If ever I did dream of such a matter, abhor me.
ROD Thou told'st me thou didst hold him in thy hate.
IAGO Despise me if I do not. Three great ones of the city,
In personal suit to make me his lieutenant,
Off-capp'd to him; and, by the faith of man,
(I know my price), I am worth no worse a place:
But he, as loving his own pride and purposes,
Evades them, with a bombast circumstance
Horribly stuff'd with epithets of war;

Dream

The Tragedy of Othello

[End of Act 5]

For they succeed on you. To you, lord governor,
Remains the censure of this hellish villain;
The time, the place, the torture. O, enforce it!
Myself will straight aboard, and to the state
This heavy act with heavy heart relate.

You Are Hell

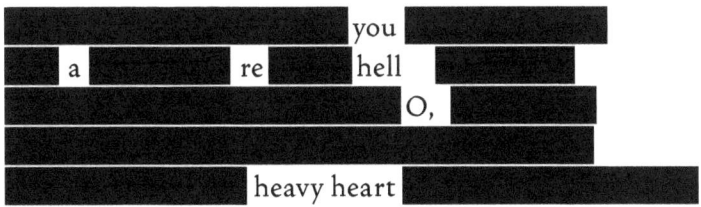

you
a   re   hell
           O,

heavy heart

Richard the Second

[End of Act 5]

With Cain go wander through shades of night,
And never show thy head by day nor light.
Lords, I protest my soul is full of woe
That blood should sprinkle me to make me grow.
Come, mourn with me for that I do lament,
And put on sullen black incontinent.
I'll make a voyage to the Holy Land
To wash this blood off from my guilty hand.
March sadly after, grace my mournings here;
In weeping after this untimely bier.

I Wander through Thy Light

i   wander through
         thy   light

                    to   grow

To wash   off   my
                mourning

The Tragedy of King Lear

[End of Act 5]

Never, never, never, never, never!
Pray you, undo this button. Thank you, sir.
(Do you see this? Look on her! look! her lips!
Look there, look there!) O, O, O, O. He dies.
EDG He faints!—My lord, my lord!
KENT Break, heart; I prithee, break!
EDG Look up, my lord.
KENT Vex not his ghost. O let him pass! He hates him much
That would upon the rack of this tough world
Stretch him out longer.
EDG He is gone. indeed.
KENT The wonder is he hath endur'd so long.
He but usurp'd his life.
Albany. Bear them from hence. Our present business
Is general woe. [To Kent and Edgar] Friends of my soul, you twain
Rule in this realm, and the gor'd state sustain.
KENT I have a journey, sir, shortly to go.
My master calls me, I must not say no.
EDG The weight of this sad time we must obey;
Speak what we feel, not what we ought to say.
The oldest hath borne most: we that are young
Shall never see so much, nor live so long.

O, O, O, O

Much Ado about Nothing

[Act 1, Scene 1]

LEON   I learn in this letter that Don Pedro of Arragon comes this night to Messina.
MESS   He is very near by this: he was not three leagues off when I left him.
LEON   How many gentlemen have you lost in this action?
MESS   But few of any sort, and none of name.
LEON   A victory is twice itself when the achiever brings home full numbers. I find here that Don Pedro hath bestowed much honour on a young Florentine called Claudio.
MESS   Much deserved on his part and equally remembered by Don Pedro: he hath borne himself beyond the promise of his age, doing in the figure of a lamb the feats of a lion: he hath indeed better bettered expectation than you must expect of me to tell you how.
LEON   He hath an uncle here in Messina will be very much glad of it.
MESS   I have already delivered him letters, and there appears much joy in him; even so

In Letters

I have lost much honour in letters

The Tragedy of Julius Caesar

[End of Act 5]

His life was gentle, and the elements
So mix'd in him that Nature might stand up
And say to all the world, 'This was a man!'
OCT   According to his virtue let us use him,
With all respect and rites of burial.
Within my tent his bones to-night shall lie,
Most like a soldier, order'd honourably.
So, call the field to rest; and let's away,
To part the glories of this happy day.

His Bones

His life was
So mix'd up
to all the world,
let us
all respect
his bones
this day.

Timon of Athens

[End of Act 5]

ALCIB 'Here lies a wretched corse, of wretched soul bereft:
Seek not my name: a plague consume you wicked caitiffs left!
Here lie I, Timon; who, alive, all living men did hate:
Pass by and curse thy fill; but pass and stay not here thy gait.'
These well express in thee thy latter spirits:
Though thou abhorr'dst in us our human griefs,
Scorn'dst our brain's flow and those our droplets which
From niggard nature fall, yet rich conceit
Taught thee to make vast Neptune weep for aye
On thy low grave, on faults forgiven. Dead
Is noble Timon, of whose memory
Hereafter more. Bring me into your city,
And I will use the olive with my sword,
Make war breed peace, make peace stint war, make each
Prescribe to other as each other's leech.
Let our drums strike.

Memory

our human griefs,
flow and our droplets
fall, yet

memory
our city,
will live

THE LIFE AND DEATH OF KING JOHN

[End of Act 5]

To the sea-side, and put his cause and quarrel
To the disposing of the cardinal:
With whom yourself, myself, and other lords,
If you think meet, this afternoon will post
To consummate this business happily.
BAST   Let it be so. And you, my noble prince,
With other princes that may best be spar'd,
Shall wait upon your father's funeral.
P HEN   At Worcester must his body be interr'd;
For so he will'd it.
BAST   Thither shall it then.
And happily may your sweet self put on
The lineal state and glory of the land!
To whom, with all submission, on my knee,
I do bequeath my faithful services
And true subjection everlastingly.
SAL   And the like tender of our love we make,
To rest without a spot for evermore.
P HEN   I have a kind soul that would give [you] thanks,
And knows not how to do it but with tears.
BAST   O, let us pay the time but needful woe,
Since it hath been beforehand with our griefs.
This England never did, nor never shall,
Lie at the proud foot of a conqueror,
But when it first did help to wound itself.
Now these her princes are come home again,
Come the three corners of the world in arms,
And we shall shock them. Nought shall make us rue,
If England to itself do rest but true.

COME HOME

If you think

the love we make

shall
conqueror
wound s
come home

And we shall make
it true.

The Two Gentlemen of Verona

[Act 1, Scene 1]

VAL Cease to persuade, my loving Proteus;
Home-keeping youth have ever homely wits.
Were't not affection chains thy tender days
To the sweet glances of thy honour'd love,
I rather would entreat thy company
To see the wonders of the world abroad
Than, living dully sluggardiz'd at home,
Wear out thy youth with shapeless idleness.
But since thou lov'st, love still and thrive therein,
Even as I would when I to love begin.
PRO Wilt thou be gone? Sweet Valentine, adieu!
Think on thy Proteus, when thou haply seest
Some rare noteworthy object in thy travel:
Wish me partaker in thy happiness
When thou dost meet good hap; and in thy danger,
If ever danger do environ thee,
Commend thy grievance to my holy prayers,
For I will be thy beadsman, Valentine.
VAL And on a love-book pray for my success?
PRO Upon some book I love I'll pray for thee.
VAL That's on some shallow story of deep love,

My Valentine

The Tragedy of Cymbeline

[Act 1, Scene 1]

1. GENT You do not meet a man but frowns: our bloods
No more obey the heavens than our courtiers
Still seem as does the king.
2. GENT But what's the matter?
1. GENT His daughter, and the heir of's kingdom, whom
He purposed to his wife's sole son—a widow
That late he married—hath referr'd herself
Unto a poor but worthy gentleman. She's wedded;
Her husband banish'd; she imprison'd: all
Is outward sorrow; though I think the king
Be touch'd at very heart.
2. GENT None but the king?
1. GENT He that hath lost her too; so is the queen,
That most desired the match; but not a courtier,
Although they wear their faces to the bent
Of the king's look's, hath a heart that is not
Glad at the thing they scowl at.
2. GENT And why so?
1. GENT He that hath miss'd the princess is a thing

The Bent Heart

You do not
obey

sorrow

but the

bent
heart

The Life of Henry the Fifth

[Epilogue]

Thus far, with rough and all-unable pen,
Our bending author hath pursu'd the story,
In little room confining mighty men,
Mangling by starts the full course of their glory.
Small time, but in that small most greatly liv'd
This star of England: Fortune made his sword;
By which the world's best garden be achiev'd,
And of it left his son imperial lord.
Henry the Sixth, in infant bands crown'd King
Of France and England, did this king succeed,
Whose state so many had the managing,
That they lost France and made his England bleed.
Which oft our stage hath shown; and, for their sake,
In your fair minds let this acceptance take.

The Garden

with rough   pen
I
                    made
   the   garden
      m y
                own

THE FIRST PART OF HENRY THE SIXTH

[End of Act 5]

KING   Whether it be through force of your report,
My noble Lord of Suffolk, or for that
My tender youth was never yet attaint
With any passion of inflaming love,
I cannot tell; but this I am assur'd,
I feel such sharp dissension in my breast,
Such fierce alarums both of hope and fear,
As I am sick with working of my thoughts.
Take, therefore, shipping; post, my lord, to France;
Agree to any covenants, and procure
That Lady Margaret do vouchsafe to come
To cross the seas to England and be crown'd
King Henry's faithful and anointed queen:
For your expenses and sufficient charge,
Among the people gather up a tenth.
Be gone, I say; for, till you do return,
I rest perplexed with a thousand cares.
And you, good uncle, banish all offence:
If you do censure me by what you were,
Not what you are, I know it will excuse
This sudden execution of my will.
And so, conduct me, where from company
I may revolve and ruminate my grief.
GLO   Ay, grief, I fear me, both at first and last.
SUF   Thus Suffolk hath prevail'd; and thus he goes,
As did the youthful Paris once to Greece,
With hope to find the like event in love,
But prosper better than the Trojan did.
Margaret shall now be queen, and rule the king;
But I will rule both her, the king, and realm.

YOUTH

youth

is

sharp　　　in my breast,

tho

it

gather

a thousand cares.

And so
I
　　　both　first and last

hope to　　　love

her

THE FIRST PART OF HENRY THE FOURTH

[End of Act 5]

That the pursuers took him. At my tent
The Douglas is, and I beseech your grace
I may dispose of him.
KING   With all my heart.
PRINCE   Then, brother John of Lancaster, to you
This honorable bounty shall belong.
Go to the Douglas, and deliver him
Up to his pleasure, ransomless and free:
His valour shown upon our crests to-day
Hath taught us how to cherish such high deeds,
Even in the bosom of our adversaries.
JOHN   I thank your grace for this high courtesy,
Which I shall give away immediately.
KING   Then this remains, that we divide our power.
You, son John, and my cousin Westmoreland
Towards York shall bend you, with your dearest speed,
To meet Northumberland and the prelate Scroop,
Who, as we hear, are busily in arms:
Myself and you, son Harry, will towards Wales,
To fight with Glendower and the Earl of March.
Rebellion in this land shall lose his sway,
Meeting the cheque of such another day,
And since this business so fair is done,
Let us not leave till all our own be won.

Another Day

                      I beseech you
With all my heart
                                to
                deliver

                                your dearest
                        arms
To
Me   another day

The First Part of Henry the Fourth

[Act 1, Scene 1]

KING So shaken as we are, so wan with care,
Find we a time for frighted peace to pant,
And breathe short-winded accents of new broils
To be commenc'd in strands afar remote.
No more the thirsty entrance of this soil
Shall daub her lips with her own children's blood,
Nor more shall trenching war channel her fields,
Nor bruise her flowerets with the armed hoofs
Of hostile paces. Those opposed eyes,
Which like the meteors of a troubled heaven,
All of one nature, of one substance bred,
Did lately meet in the intestine shock
And furious close of civil butchery,
Shall now in mutual well-beseeming ranks
March all one way, and be no more oppos'd

Shaken

shaken as we are,
we
breathe

bruise

And
Shall
be no more

Love's Labour's Lost

[Act 1, Scene 1]

KING Let fame, that all hunt after in their lives,
Live register'd upon our brazen tombs,
And then grace us in the disgrace of death;
When, spite of cormorant devouring Time,
The endeavor of this present breath may buy
That honour which shall bate his scythe's keen edge,
And make us heirs of all eternity.
Therefore, brave conquerors,—for so you are,
That war against your own affections
And the huge army of the world's desires,—
Our late edict shall strongly stand in force:
Navarre shall be the wonder of the world;
Our court shall be a little academe,
Still and contemplative in living art.
You three, Berowne, Dumaine, and Longaville,
Have sworn for three years' term to live with me,
My fellow-scholars, and to keep those statutes
That are recorded in this schedule here:
Your oaths are pass'd; and now subscribe your names,
That his own hand may strike his honour down
That violates the smallest branch herein.

Time

Let

Time

make us heirs of

our own affections
And the world

record
our names

The Tragedy of Macbeth

[End of Act 5]

That fled the snares of watchful tyranny,
Producing forth the cruel ministers
Of this dead butcher and his fiend-like queen,
Who, as 'tis thought, by self and violent hands
Took off her life—this, and what needful else
That calls upon us, by the grace of Grace
We will perform in measure, time and place.
So, thanks to all at once and to each one,
Whom we invite to see us crown'd at Scone.
Flourish.

The Snares of Life

The Famous History of the Life of King Henry the Eighth

[Epilogue]

'Tis ten to one, this play can never please
All that are here. Some come to take their ease,
And sleep an act or two; but those, we fear,
We have frighted with our trumpets; so, 'tis clear,
They'll say 'tis naught: others, to hear the city
Abused extremely, and to cry 'That's witty!'
Which we have not done neither: that, I fear,
All the expected good we're like to hear
For this play at this time, is only in
The merciful construction of good women;
For such a one we show'd 'em: if they smile,
And say 'twill do, I know, within a while
All the best men are ours; for 'tis ill hap
If they hold when their ladies bid 'em clap.

Such Art

Some come

to cry
t o   fear,
       to hear

The   construction of
   such

      ar   t

The Tragedy of King John

[Act 1, Scene 1]

K. JOHN Now, say, Chatillion, what would France with us?
CHAT Thus, after greeting, speaks the King of France,
In my behaviour, to the majesty,
The borrow'd majesty, of England here.
Eli. A strange beginning: 'borrow'd majesty'!
K. JOHN Silence, good mother; hear the embassy.
CHAT Philip of France, in right and true behalf
Of thy deceased brother Goeffrey's son,
Arthur Plantagenet, lays most lawful claim
To this fair island and the territories,
To Ireland, Poitiers, Anjou, Touraine, Maine;
Desiring thee to lay aside the sword
Which sways usurpingly these several titles,
And put these same into young Arthur's hand,
Thy nephew and right royal sovereign.
K. JOHN What follows if we disallow of this?
CHAT The proud control of fierce and bloody war,

Silence

Now
speak
to the
beginning:
Silence

What follows if we disallow this?

The Merchant of Venice

[Act 1, Scene 1]

ANT In sooth, I know not why I am so sad:
It wearies me; you say it wearies you;
But how I caught it, found it, or came by it,
What stuff 'tis made of, whereof it is born,
I am to learn;
And such a want-wit sadness makes of me,
That I have much ado to know myself.
SALAR Your mind is tossing on the ocean;
There, where your argosies with portly sail,—
Like signiors and rich burghers on the flood,
Or, as it were, the pageants of the sea—
Do overpeer the petty traffickers,
That curtsy to them, do them reverence,
As they fly by them with their woven wings.
SALAN Believe me, sir, had I such venture forth,
The better part of my affections would
Be with my hopes abroad. I should be still
Plucking the grass to know where sits the wind;
Peering in maps for ports and piers and roads;
And every object that might make me fear
Misfortunes to my ventures out of doubt

Sadness

I know not why

sadness

is tossing

my hopes to the wind

A Comedy of Errors

[End of Act 5]

DRO. S Not I, sir; you are my elder.
DRO. E That's a question: how shall we try it?
DRO. S We'll draw cuts for the senior: till then lead thou first.
DRO. E Nay, then, thus:
We came into the world like brother and brother;
And now let's go hand in hand, not one before another.

A Question

you are
a question: how shall we
draw
the world
hand in hand

The Tragedy of Hamlet, Prince of Denmark

[End of Act 5]

And from his mouth whose voice will draw on more;
But let this same be presently perform'd,
Even while men's minds are wild, lest more mischance
On plots and errors, happen.
FORT   Let four captains
Bear Hamlet, like a soldier, to the stage;
For he was likely, had he been put on,
To have prov'd most royal. And for his passage
The soldiers' music and the rites of war
Speak loudly for him!
Take up the bodies. Such a sight as this
Becomes the field, but here shows much amiss.
Go, bid the soldiers shoot.

Wild Like Music

his mouth
be
wild,

like

music
loud

but   much amiss.

The Lamentable Tragedy of Titus Andronicus

[Act 1, Scene 1]

SAT   Noble patricians, patrons of my right,
Defend the justice of my cause with arms;
And, countrymen, my loving followers,
Plead my successive title with your swords:
I am his first-born son, that was the last
That wore the imperial diadem of Rome;
Then let my father's honours live in me,
Nor wrong mine age with this indignity.
BAS   Romans, friends, followers, favourers of my right,
If ever Bassianus, Caesar's son,
Were gracious in the eyes of royal Rome,
Keep then this passage to the Capitol,
And suffer not dishonour to approach
The imperial seat, to virtue consecrate,
To justice, continence, and nobility;

Loving Words

The First Part of Henry the Sixth

[Act 1, Scene 1]

BED   Hung be the heavens with black, yield day to night!
Comets, importing change of times and states,
Brandish your crystal tresses in the sky,
And with them scourge the bad revolting stars,
That have consented unto Henry's death!
King Henry the Fifth, too famous to live long!
England ne'er lost a king of so much worth.
GLO   England ne'er had a king until his time.
Virtue he had, deserving to command:
His brandish'd sword did blind men with his beams;
His arms spread wider than a dragon's wings;
His sparking eyes, replete with wrathful fire,
More dazzled and drove back his enemies
Than mid-day sun fierce bent against their faces.
What should I say? his deeds exceed all speech:

WIDER

your

death

is

wider than a dragon's wings
replete with a
dazzled
sun

The Taming of the Shrew

[Act 1, Scene 1]

SLY I'll pheeze you, in faith.
HOSTESS A pair of stocks, you rogue!
SLY Y'are a baggage: the Slys are no rogues; look
In the chronicles; we came in with Richard Conqueror.
Therefore, paucas pallabris; let the world slide. Sessa!
HOSTESS You will not pay for the glasses you have burst?
SLY No, not a denier. Go, by St. Jeronimy, go to thy cold bed, and warm thee.
HOSTESS I know my remedy: I must go fetch the third-borough.

[Hostess exits]

SLY Third or fourth or fifth borough, I'll answer him by law: I'll not budge an inch, boy: let him come and kindly.

[Falls asleep]

Remedy

the world's a

cold bed

and warm

remedy: I must

Fall asleep

The Most Excellent and Lamentable Tragedy of Romeo and Juliet

[Prologue]

Two households both alike in dignity
(In fair Verona, where we lay our scene)
From ancient grudge break to new mutiny,
Where civil blood makes civil hands unclean.
From forth the fatal loins of these two foes
A pair of star-cross'd lovers take their life,
Whose misadventur'd piteous overthrows
Do with their death bury their parents' strife.
The fearful passage of their death-mark'd love
And the continuance of their parents' rage
(Which, but their children's end, nought could remove)
Is now the two hours' traffic of our stage,
The which if you with patient ears attend
What here shall miss, our toil shall strive to mend.

Both Like

Section Two

Exeunt

The Tempest

> [Act 1, Scene 1]

MASTER Boatswain!
BOATSWAIN Here, Master! What cheer?
MASTER Good. Speak to th' mariners. Fall to't, yarely, or we run ourselves aground—bestir! bestir!

> [Exit]
> [Enter Mariners]

BOATSWAIN Heigh, my hearts! Cheerly, cheerly, my hearts! Yare, yare! Take in the topsail! Tend to th' Master's whistle! Blow, till thou burst thy wind, if
room enough!

> [Enter Alonso, Sebastian, Antonio, Ferdinand, Gonzalo, and others]

ALONSO Good boatswain, have care. Where's the master? Play the men!
BOATSWAIN I pray now, keep below.

Bestir

The Tragedy of King Lear

[Act 1, Scene 1]

KENT   I thought the king had more affected the Duke of Albany than Cornwall.

GLO   It did always seem so to us; but now, in the division of the kingdom, it appears not which of the dukes he values most, for equalities are so weighed, that curiosity in neither can make choice of either's moiety.

KENT   Is not this your son, my lord?

GLO   His breeding, sir, hath been at my charge: I have so often blushed to acknowledge him, that now I am brazed to it.

KENT   I cannot conceive you.

GLO   Sir, this young fellow's mother could: whereupon she grew round-wombed, and had, indeed, sir, a son for her cradle ere she had a husband for her bed. Do you smell a fault?

KENT   I cannot wish the fault undone, the issue of it being so proper.

GLO   But I have, sir, a son by order of law, some

Curiosity

curiosity

bred

a

round-womb   and   a   cradle
          Do you
     wish the fault undone

The Tragedy of King Richard the Second

[Act 1, Scene 1]

KING RICHARD Old John of Gaunt, time-honour'd Lancaster,
Hast thou, according to thy oath and band,
Brought hither Henry Herford, thy bold son,
Here to make good the boist'rous late appeal—
Which then our leisure would not let us hear—
Against the Duke of Norfolk, Thomas Mowbray?
GAUNT I have, my liege.
KING RICHARD Tell me, moreover, hast thou sounded him,
If he appeal the duke on ancient malice,
Or worthily, as a good subject should,
On some known ground of treachery in him?

The Sound Ancient

Old   time

let us hear
the

sound
ancient
as a good subject should

The Comedy of Errors

[Act 1, Scene 1]

MERCH   Proceed, Solinus, to procure my fall,
And by the doom of death end woes and all.
DUKE   Merchant of Syracusa, plead no more.
I am not partial to infringe our laws:
The enmity and discord which of late
Sprung from the rancorous outrage of your duke
To merchants, our well-dealing countrymen,
Who wanting guilders to redeem their lives,
Have seal'd his rigorous statutes with their bloods,
Excludes all pity from our threat'ning looks.
For, since the mortal and intestine jars
'Twixt thy seditious countrymen and us,
It hath in solemn synods been decreed,
Both by the Syracusians and ourselves,
To admit no traffic to our adverse towns:
Nay, more, if any, born at Ephesus,
Be seen at any Syracusian marts and fairs;
Again: if any Syracusian born
Come to the bay of Ephesus: he dies,
His goods confiscate to the duke's dispose;

Proceed

Proceed to

part

from your

lives,

pity our
mortal

selves,

born
to die

The Tragedy of Troilus and Cressida

[Prologue]

In Troy, there lies the scene. From isles of Greece
The princes orgillous, their high blood chaf'd,
Have to the port of Athens sent their ships,
Fraught with the ministers and instruments
Of cruel war. Sixty-and-nine, that wore
Their crownets regal, from th' Athenian bay
Put forth toward Phrygia and their vow is made
To ransack Troy, within whose strong immures
The ravish'd Helen, Menelaus' queen,
With wanton Paris sleeps, and that's the quarrel.
To Tenedos they come,
And the deep-drawing [barks] do there disgorge
Their warlike fraughtage. Now on Dardan plains
The fresh and yet unbruised Greeks do pitch
Their brave pavilions. Priam's six-gated city,
Dardan and Timbria, Helias, Chetas, Troien,
And Antenonides, with massy staples
And corresponsive and fulfilling bolts,
[Sperr] up the sons of Troy.
Now expectation, tickling skittish spirits,

Expectation

King Henry the Sixth, Part Three

[End of Act 5]

Reignier, her father, to the king of France:
Hath pawn'd the Sicils and Jerusalem,
And hither have they sent it for her ransom.
KING Away with her, and waft her hence to France.
And now what rests but that we spend the time
With stately triumphs, mirthful comic shows,
Such as befits the pleasure of the court?
Sound drums and trumpets! farewell sour annoy!
For here, I hope, begins our lasting joy.

Our Lasting Joy

i
have sent for

mirthful

drums and trumpets
For our lasting joy.

A Midsummer Night's Dream

[Act 1, Scene 1]

THE   Now, fair Hippolyta, our nuptial hour
Draws on apace: four happy days bring in
Another moon; but, O! methinks, how slow
This old moon wanes; she lingers my desires,
Like to a step-dame, or a dowager
Long withering out a young man's revenue.
HIP   Four days will quickly steep themselves in night;
Four nights will quickly dream away the time;
And then the moon, like to a silver bow
New-bent in heaven, shall behold the night
Of our solemnities.
THE   Go, Philostrate,
Stir up the Athenian youth to merriments;
Awake the pert and nimble spirit of mirth;
Turn melancholy forth to funerals;
The pale companion is not for our pomp.

[Exit Philostrate]

Hippolyta, I woo'd thee with my sword,
And won thy love, doing thee injuries;
But I will wed thee in another key,
With pomp, with triumph and with revelling.

Spirit of Mirth

our
day
wanes; desires
will quickly steep themselves in night;

Awake spirit of mirth;

with
thy love
I will
revel

Measure for Measure

DUKE Escalus.
ESCALUS My lord.
DUKE Of government the properties to unfold,
Would seem in me t' affect speech and discourse;
Since I am put to know that your own science
Exceeds, in that, the lists of all advice
My strength can give you. Then no more remains,
But that to your sufficiency as your worth is able,
And let them work. The nature of our people,
Our city's institutions, and the terms
For common justice, y' are as pregnant in
As art and practice hath enriched any
That we remember. There is our commission,
From which we would not have you warp. Call hither,
I say, bid come before us Angelo.

[Exit an Attendant]

What figure of us think you he will bear?
For you must know, we have with special soul
Elected him our absence to supply,

Speech

speech
Exceeds
strength
so
let

art   enrich
our

soul

The Life of Timon of Athens

[Act 1, Scene 1]

POET   Good day, sir.
PAIN   I am glad you're well.
POET   I have not seen you long: how goes the world?
PAIN   It wears, sir, as it grows.
POET   Ay, that's well known:
But what particular rarity? what strange,
Which manifold record not matches? See,
Magic of bounty! all these spirits thy power
Hath conjured to attend. I know the merchant.
PAIN   I know them both; th' other's a jeweller.
Merch. O, 'tis a worthy lord!
JEW   Nay, that's most fix'd.
MERCH   A most incomparable man, breath'd, as it were,
To an untirable and continuate goodness:
He passes.
JEW   I have a jewel here—
MERCH   O, pray, let's see't: for the Lord Timon, sir?

Good Day, Pain

Good day
PAIN
           you

                    strange,

Magic

          goodness

Troilus and Cressida

[End of Act 5]

Though not for me, yet for your aching bones.
Brethren and sisters of the hold-door trade,
Some two months hence my will shall here be made.
It should be now, but that my fear is this:
Some galled goose of Winchester would hiss.
Till then I'll sweat and seek about for eases,
And at that time bequeath you my diseases.

Seek

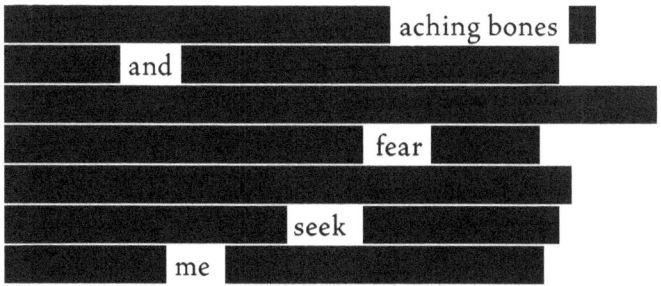

aching bones
and
fear
seek
me

The Two Gentlemen of Verona

[End of Act 5]

To which I thus subscribe: Sir Valentine,
Thou art a gentleman and well deriv'd;
Take thou thy Silvia, for thou hast deserv'd her.
VAL   I thank your Grace; the gift hath made me happy.
I now beseech you, for your daughter's sake,
To grant one boom that I shall ask of you.
DUKE   I grant it, for thine own, whate'er it be.
VAL   These banish'd men that I have kept withal
Are men endued with worthy qualities:
Forgive them what they have committed here,
And let them be recall'd from their exile.
They are reformed, civil, full of good,
And fit for great employment, worthy lord.
DUKE   Thou hast prevail'd; I pardon them, and thee;
Dispose of them as thou know'st their deserts.
Come, let us go; we will include all jars
With triumphs, mirth and rare solemnity.
VAL   And as we walk along, I dare be bold
With our discourse to make your Grace to smile.
What think you of this page, my lord?
DUKE   I think the boy hath grace in him; he blushes.
VAL   I warrant you, my lord, more grace than boy.
DUKE   What mean you by that saying?
VAL   Please you, I'll tell you as we pass along,
That you will wonder what hath fortuned.
Come, Proteus; 'tis your penance but to hear
The story of your loves discovered;
That done, our day of marriage shall be yours;
One feast, one house, one mutual happiness.

We Will Dare

The Tragedy of Cymbeline

[End of Act 5]

For many years thought dead, are now reviv'd,
To the majestic cedar join'd, whose issue
Promises Britain peace and plenty.
CYM   Well;
My peace we will begin. And, Caius Lucius,
Although the victor, we submit to Caesar,
And to the Roman empire; promising
To pay our wonted tribute, from the which
We were dissuaded by our wicked queen;
Whom heavens, in justice, both on her and hers—
Have laid most heavy hand.
SOOTH   The fingers of the powers above do tune
The harmony of this peace. The vision,
Which I made known to Lucius, ere the stroke
Of this yet scarce-cold battle, at this instant
Is full accomplish'd; for the Roman eagle,
From south to west on wing soaring aloft,
Lessen'd herself, and in the beams o' the sun
So vanish'd: which foreshow'd our princely eagle,
The imperial Caesar, should again unite
His favour with the radiant Cymbeline,
Which shines here in the west.
CYM   Laud we the gods;
And let our crooked smokes climb to their nostrils
From our blest altars. Publish we this peace
To all our subjects. Set we forward: let
A Roman and a British ensign wave
Friendly together; so through Lud's town march:
And in the temple of great Jupiter
Our peace we'll ratify; seal it with feasts.
Set on there! Never was a war did cease,
Ere bloody hands were wash'd, with such a peace.

Our Crooked Temple

we will submit to this instant From south to west in the beams o' the sun which should let our crooked temple b e wash'd with peace.

The Play of Pericles, Prince of Tyre

[Prologue]

To sing a song that old was sung,
From ashes ancient Gower is come,
Assuming man's infirmities,
To glad your ear, and please your eyes.
It hath been sung at festivals,
On ember-eves, and holy-ales;
And lords and ladies in their lives
Have read it for restoratives:
The purchase is to make men glorious;
Et bonum quo antiquius, eo melius.
If you, born in these latter times,
When wit's more ripe, accept my rimes,
And that to hear an old man sing
May to your wishes pleasure bring,
I life would wish, and that I might
Waste it for you like taper-light.
This Antioch, then, Antiochus the Great
Built up, this city, for his chiefest seat,
The fairest in all Syria,
I tell you what mine authors say.
This king unto him took a fere,
Who died and left a female heir,
So buxom, blithe, and full of face
As heaven had lent her all his grace;

Glorious

To sing a song
From ashes

To your eyes

is to make men glorious

and

died
blithe

The Tragedy of Romeo and Juliet

[End of Act 5]

PRINCE   A glooming peace this morning with it brings,
The sun for sorrow will not show his head.
Go hence to have more talk of these sad things:
Some shall be pardon'd, and some punished.
For never was a story of more woe
Than this of Juliet and her Romeo.

This Morning

                         this morning   brings
The sun   not
              more   sad things
              and
              more woe

All's Well that Ends Well

[End of Act 5]

All yet seems well; and if it end so meet,
The bitter past, more welcome is the sweet.
Flourish.

[Epilogue—Spoken by the King]

The king's a beggar, now the play is done:
All is well ended if this suit be won
That you express content; which we will pay,
With strife to please you, day exceeding day:
Ours be your patience then, and yours our parts;
Your gentle hands lend us, and take our hearts.

Take Heart

if it

is done
well
express content
With
your art
and take heart

Measure for Measure

[End of Act 5]

Thanks, good friend Escalus, for thy much goodness:
There's more behind that is more gratulate.
Thanks, Provost, for thy care and secrecy;
We shill employ thee in a worthier place.
Forgive him, Angelo, that brought you home
The head of Ragozine for Claudio's:
The offence pardons itself. Dear Isabel,
I have a motion much imports your good,
Whereto if you'll a willing ear incline,
What's mine is yours, and what is yours is mine.
So, bring us to our palace, where we'll show
What's yet behind, that's meet you all should know.

531 behind to come. gratulate pleasing. 537 motion proposal.

Thanks

Thanks   for thy
         behind
              for thy

                              good

         behind, that's   s o

                    pleasing

As You Like It

[Epilogue]

and good plays prove the better by the help of good epilogues. What a case am I in then, that am neither a good epilogue nor cannot insinuate with you in the behalf of a good play. I am not furnished like a beggar; therefore to beg will not become me: my way is to conjure you, and I'll begin with the women. I charge you, O women, for the love you bear to men, to like as much of this play as please you. And I charge you, O men, for the love you bear to women—as I perceive by your simp'ring, none of you hates them— that between you and the women the play may please. If I were a woman I would kiss as many of you as had beards that pleas'd me, complexions that liked me and breaths that I defied not. And I am sure as many as have good beards or good faces or sweet breaths will, for my kind offer, when I make curtsy, bid me farewell.

My Kind Offer

The Second Part of King Henry the Fourth, the Induction

RUM   Open your ears; for which of you will stop
The vent of hearing when loud Rumour speaks?
I, from the orient to the drooping west,
Making the wind my post-horse, still unfold
The acts commenced on this ball of earth:
Upon my tongues continual slanders ride,
The which in every language I pronounce,
Stuffing the ears of men with false reports.
I speak of peace, while covert enmity
Under the smile of safety wounds the world:
And who but Rumour, who but only I,
Make fearful musters and prepared defence,
Whiles the big year, swoln with some other grief,
Is thought with child by the stern tyrant war,
And no such matter? Rumour is a pipe
Blown by surmises, jealousies, conjectures,
And of so easy and so plain a stop
That the blunt monster with uncounted heads,
The still-discordant wavering multitude,
Can play upon it. But what need I thus
My well-known body to anatomize
Among my household? Why is Rumour here?

Blunt Monster

Open your ears

I

unfold

my tongue
in every language

I speak
the smile of

grief,

That blunt monster

The Tragedy of Macbeth

[Act 1, Scene 1]

1 WITCH   When shall we three meet again
In thunder, lightning, or in rain?
2 WITCH   When the hurlyburly's done,
When the battle's lost and won.3
3 WITCH   That will be ere the set of sun.
1 WITCH   Where the place?
2 WITCH   Upon the heath.
3 WITCH   There to meet with Macbeth.
1 WITCH   I come, Graymalkin!
2 WITCH   Paddock calls.
3 WITCH   Anon!
All. Fair is foul, and foul is fair:
Hover through the fog and filthy air.

When

The Tragedy of Coriolanus

[Act 1, Scene 1]

1 CIT   Before we proceed any further, hear me speak.
ALL   Speak, speak.
1 CIT   You are all resolved rather to die than to famish?
ALL   Resolved, resolved.
1 CIT   First, you know Caius Marcius is chief enemy to the people.
ALL   We know't, we know't.
1 CIT   Let us kill him, and we'll have corn at our own price. Is't a verdict?
ALL   No more talking on't; let it be done. Away, away!
2 CIT   One word, good citizens.
1 CIT   We are accounted poor citizens, the patricians good. What authority surfeits on would relieve us. If they would yield us but the superfluity, while it were wholesome, we might guess they relieved us humanely; but they think we are too dear: the leanness that afflicts us, the object of our misery, is as an inventory to particularise their abundance;

Before We Speak

Before we
speak

we'll have

No more talking
good
poor citizens

The Winter's Tale

[End of Act 5]

As I thought dead, and have in vain said many
A prayer upon her grave. I'll not seek far,—
For him, I partly know his mind,—to find thee
An honourable husband. Come, Camillo,
And take her by the hand, whose worth and honesty
Is richly noted, and here justified
By us, a pair of kings. Let's from this place.
What! look upon my brother: both your pardons,
That e'er I put between your holy looks
My ill suspicion. This is your son-in-law,
And son unto the king,—whom heavens directing,
Is troth-plight to your daughter. Good Paulina,
Lead us from hence, where we may leisurely
Each one demand an answer to his part
Perform'd in this wide gap of time since first
We were dissever'd: hastily lead away.

In Vain

I have in vain said
I'll find
the
answer to
time

Twelfth Night

[End of Act 5]

But when I came to man's estate,
With hey, ho, the wind and the rain,
'Gainst knaves and thieves men shut their gate,
For the rain it raineth every day.
But when I came, alas, to wive,
With hey, ho, the wind and the rain,
By swaggering could I never thrive,
For the rain it raineth every day.
But when I came unto my beds,
With hey, ho, the wind and the rain,
With tosspots still had drunken heads,
For the rain it raineth every day.
A great while ago the world begun,
With hey, ho, the wind and the rain:
But that's all one, our play is done,
And we'll strive to please you every day.

I Rain

when

it raineth
I
rain,

when

it raineth every day
i
rain
But
strive to please you

The Tragedy of Titus Andronicus

[End of Act 5]

AAR   O, why should wrath be mute, and fury dumb?
I am no baby, I, that with base prayers
I should repent the evils I have done.
Ten thousand worse than ever yet I did
Would I perform, if I might have my will:
If one good deed in all my life I did,
I do repent it from my very soul.
LUC   Some loving friends convey the emperor hence,
And give him burial in his father's grave.
My father and Lavinia shall forthwith
Be closed in our household's monument.
As for that heinous tiger, Tamora,
No funeral rite, nor man in mournful weeds!
No mournful bell shall ring her burial;
But throw her forth to beasts and birds of prey.
Her life was beast-like, and devoid of pity;
And, being so, shall have like want of pity.
See justice done on Aaron, that damn'd Moor,
By whom our heavy haps had their beginning:
Then, afterwards, to order well the state,
That like events may ne'er it ruinate.

HER

I, with

all my life

lov e the

tiger

th e beasts and
Her

The Merchant of Venice

[End of Act 5]

But were the day come, I should wish it dark,
That I were couching with the doctor's clerk.
Well, while I live I'll fear no other thing
So sore as keeping safe Nerissa's ring.

Keep Safe

the day is dark
with
fear
keep safe

Antony and Cleopatra

[End of Act 5]

CAESAR   Poison'd, then.
1 GUARD   O Caesar!
This Charmian liv'd but now; she stood and spake:
I found her trimming up the diadem
On her dead mistress; tremblingly she stood,
And on the sudden dropp'd.
CAESAR   O noble weakness!
If they had swallow'd poison, 'twould appear
By external swelling: but she looks like sleep,
As she would catch another Antony
In her strong toil of grace.
DOLABELLA   Here, on her breast,
There is a vent of blood and something blown;
The like is on her arm.
1 GUARD   This is an aspic's trail,
And these fig leaves have slime upon them, such
As th' aspic leaves upon the caves of Nile.
CAESAR   Most probable
That so she died: for her physician tells me
She hath pursu'd conclusions infinite
Of easy ways to die. Take up her bed,
And bear her women from the monument.
She shall be buried by her Antony.
No grave upon the earth shall clip in it
A pair so famous. High events as these
Strike those that make them; and their story is
No less in pity than his glory which
Brought them to be lamented. Our army shall,
In solemn show attend this funeral,
And then to Rome. Come, Dolabella, see
High order in this great solemnity.

Infinite Ways

O she stood and spake

and

pursu'd   infinite
ways to
bear her

story

The Tragedy of Richard the Third

[Act 1, Scene 1]

RICH   Now is the winter of our discontent
Made glorious summer by this sun of York;
And all the clouds that lour'd upon our house
In the deep bosom of the ocean buried.
Now are our brows bound with victorious wreaths;
Our bruised arms hung up for monuments;
Our stern alarums changed to merry meetings;
Our dreadful marches to delightful measures.
Grim-visaged war hath smooth'd his wrinkled front;
And now—instead of mounting barbed steeds,
To fright the souls of fearful adversaries,—
He capers nimbly in a lady's chamber
To the lascivious pleasing of a lute.
But I, that am not shaped for sportive tricks,
Nor made to court an amorous looking-glass;
I, that am rudely stamp'd, and want love's majesty
To strut before a wanton ambling nymph;

The Clouds

all the clouds

are
bruised

And barbed

But not shaped for tricks,

I want love

The Tragedy of Coriolanus

[End of Act 5]

Provok'd by him, you cannot,—the great danger
Which this man's life did owe you, you'll rejoice
That he is thus cut off. Please it your honours
To call me to your senate, I'll deliver
Myself your loyal servant, or endure
Your heaviest censure.
1 LORD   Bear from hence his body;
And mourn you for him! Let him be regarded
As the most noble corse that ever herald
Did follow to his urn.
2 LORD   His own impatience
Takes from Aufidius a great part of blame.
Let's make the best of it.
AUF   My rage is gone,
And I am struck with sorrow. Take him up:
Help, three o' the chiefest soldiers; I'll be one.
Beat thou the drum, that it speak mournfully;
Trail your steel pikes. Though in this city he
Hath widow'd and unchilded many a one,
Which to this hour bewail the injury,
Yet he shall have a noble memory.

The Best of It

All's Well That Ends Well

[Act 1, Scene 1]

COUNT In delivering my son from me, I bury a second husband.
BER And I, in going, madam, weep o'er my father's death anew; but I must attend his majesty's command, to whom I am now inward, evermore in subjection.
LAF You shall find of the king a husband, madam; you, sir, a father. He that so generally is at all times good must of necessity hold his virtue to you, whose worthiness would stir it up where it wanted rather than lack it where there is such abundance.
COUNT What hope is there of his majesty's amendment?
LAF He hath abandoned his physicians, madam, under whose practices he hath persecuted time with hope, and finds no other advantage in the process but only the losing of hope by time.

HOPE

I bury
death
but I must now

find

hope

with hope, and
hope

As You Like It

[Act 1, Scene 1]

ORLANDO As I remember, Adam, it was upon this Fashion bequeathed me by will but poor a thousand crowns, and, as thou sayest, charged my brother on his blessing, to breed me well: and there begins my sadness. My brother Jaques he keeps at school, and report speaks goldenly of his profit. For my part, he keeps me rustically at home, or—to speak more properly—stays me here at home unkept, for call you that keeping for a gentleman of my birth that differs not from the stalling of an ox? His horses are bred better; for, besides that they are fair with their feeding, they are taught their manage, and to that end riders dearly hir'd. But I, his brother, gain nothing under him but growth, for the which his animals on his dunghills are as much bound to him as I. Besides this nothing that he so plentifully gives me, the something that nature gave me, his countenance seems to take from me.

This Nothing

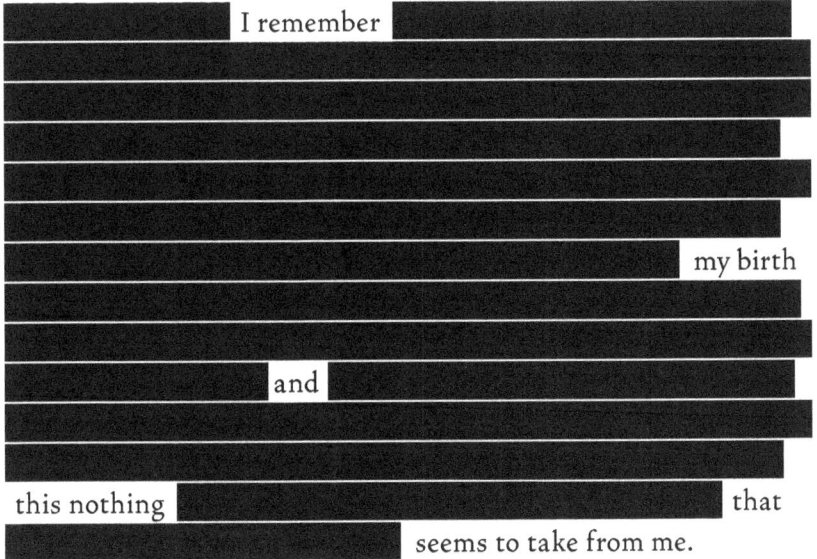

The Tragedy of Hamlet, Prince of Denmark

[Act 1, Scene 1]

BER Who's there?
FRAN Nay, answer me: stand, and unfold yourself.
BER Long live the king!
FRAN Bernardo?
BER He.
FRAN You come most carefully upon your hour.
BER 'Tis now struck twelve; get thee to bed, Francisco.
FRAN For this relief much thanks; 'tis bitter cold,
And I am sick at heart.
BER Have you had quiet guard?
FRAN Not a mouse stirring.
BER Well, good night.
If you do meet Horatio and Marcellus,
The rivals of my watch, bid them make haste.

[Enter Horatio and Marcellus]

FRAN I think I hear them. Stand, ho! Who is there?
HOR Friends to this ground.
MAR And liegemen to the Dane.

I Hear Them

King Henry the Fourth

[Part 2, Epilogue]

author will continue the story, with Sir John in it, and make you merry with fair Katharine of France: where, for any thing I know, Falstaff shall die of a sweat, unless already a' be killed with your hard opinions; for Oldcastle died a martyr, and this is not the man. My tongue is weary; when my legs are too, I will bid you good night: and so kneel down before you; but, indeed, to pray for the queen.

Pray

will　　　　　　　　　　　i　　make you
merry
　　　　　　　　　　　　　　　　　with

My tongue　　　　　　　　I will
　　　　kneel down before you　　to pray

The Merry Wives of Windsor

[Act 1, Scene 1]

[Enter Justice Shallow, Slender, [and] Sir Hugh Evans; (and later) Master Page, Falstaff, Bardolph, Nym, Pistol, Anne Page, Mistress Ford, Mistress Page, (and) Simple.]

SHAL Sir Hugh, persuade me not; I will make a Star-chamber matter of it; if he were twenty Sir John Falstaffs, he shall not abuse Robert Shallow, esquire.
SLEN In the county of Gloucester, justice of Peace, and *coram*.
SHAL Ay, cousin Slender, and *cust-alorum*.
SLEN Ay, and rato-lorum too; and a gentleman born, Master Parson; who writes himself *armigero*, in any bill, warrant, quittance, or obligation—*armigero*.
SHAL Ay, that I do; and have done any time these three hundred years.
SLEN All his successors gone before him hath done't; and all his ancestors that come after him may: they may give the dozen white luces in their coat.
SHAL It is an old coat.

O Page

THE LIFE OF HENRY THE FIFTH

[Prologue]

O for a Muse of fire, that would ascend
The brightest heaven of invention,
A kingdom for a stage, princes to act,
And monarchs to behold the swelling scene!
Then should the warlike Harry, like himself,
Assume the port of Mars, and at his heels,
Leash'd in like hounds, should famine, sword, and fire
Crouch for employment. But pardon, and gentles all,
The flat unraised spirits that have dar'd
On this unworthy scaffold to bring forth
So great an object: can this cockpit hold
The vasty fields of France? Or may we cram
Within this wooden O the very casques
That did affright the air at Agincourt?
O, pardon! since a crooked figure may
Attest in little place a million,
And let us, ciphers to this great accompt,
On your imaginary forces work.
Suppose within the girdle of these walls
Are now confined two mighty monarchies,

Within

O   Muse of fire,

can this cock

cram

Within this   very

little place

The Third Part of Henry the Sixth, with the Death of the Duke of York

[Act 1, Scene 1]

WAR   I wonder how the king escap'd our hands.
YORK   While we pursued the horsemen of the north,
He slily stole away and left his men:
Whereat the great Lord of Northumberland,
Whose warlike ears could never brook retreat,
Cheer'd up the drooping army; and himself,
Lord Clifford and Lord Stafford, all abreast,
Charged our main battle's front, and breaking in
Were by the swords of common soldiers slain.
EDW   Lord Stafford's father, Duke of Buckingham,
Is either slain or wounded dangerously;
I cleft his beaver with a downright blow:
That this is true, father, behold his blood.

[Showing his bloody sword]

MONT   And, brother, here's the Earl of Wiltshire's blood,
Whom I encounter'd as the battles join'd.
RICH   Speak thou for me, and tell them what I did.

[Throwing down the Duke of Somerset's head]

WHAT I DID

LOVE'S LABOUR'S LOST

[End of Act 5]

"When shepherds pipe on oaten straws,
And merry larks are ploughmen's clocks,
When turtles tread, and rooks, and daws,
And maiden's bleach their summer smocks,
The cuckoo then, on every tree,
Mocks married men; for thus sings he,
Cuckoo;
Cuckoo, cuckoo: O, word of fear,
Unpleasing to a married ear!"
Winter.
"When icicles hang by the wall,
And Dick the shepherd blows his nail,
And Tom bears logs into the hall,
And milk comes frozen home in pail,
When blood is nipp'd and ways be foul,
Then nightly sings the staring owl,
Tu-who;
Tu-whit, tu-who—a merry note,
While greasy Joan doth keel the pot.
When all aloud the wind doth blow,
And coughing drowns the parson's saw,
And birds sit brooding in the snow,
And Marian's nose looks red and raw,
When roasted crabs hiss in the bowl,
Then nightly sings the staring owl,
Tu-who;
Tu-whit; tu-who, a merry note,
While greasy Joan doth keel the pot."
ARM   The words of Mercury are harsh after
the songs of Apollo. You, that way: we, this way.

Milk

The Tempest

[Epilogue]

Now my charms are all o'erthrown,
And what strength I have's mine own,
Which is most faint: now, 'tis true,
I must be here confined by you,
Or sent to Naples. Let me not,
Since I have my dukedom got
And pardon'd the deceiver, dwell
In this bare island by your spell,
But release me from my bands
With the help of your good hands!
Gentle breath of yours my sails
Must fill, or else my project fails,
Which was to please. Now I want
Spirits to enforce, art to enchant,
And my ending is despair
Unless I be reliev'd by prayer
Which pierces so that it assaults
Mercy itself and frees all faults.
As you from crimes would pardon'd be,
Let your indulgence set me free.

Release Me

Now
                        'tis true,
                        you
   have
                 your spell,
But release me
With the help of your hands!
                      I want
          to
     be reliev'd
    and
                set free.

Play of Pericles, Prince of Tyre

[End of Act 5]

In Antiochus and his daughter you have heard
Of monstrous lust the due and just reward:
In Pericles, his queen and daughter, seen—
Although assail'd with fortune fierce and keen—
Virtue preserv'd from fell destruction's blast,
Led on by heaven, and crown'd with joy at last.
In Helicanus may you well descry
A figure of truth, of faith, of loyalty.
In reverend Cerimon there well appears
The worth that learned charity aye wears.
For wicked Cleon and his wife, when fame
Had spread their cursed deed, and honour'd name
Of Pericles, to rage the city turn,
That him and his they in his palace burn:
The gods for murder seemed so content
To punish; although not done, but meant.
So on your patience evermore attending,
New joy wait on you! Here our play has ending.

Evermore Joy

you have heard
Of monstrous
and
fierce
destruction

may you

spread   no
rage

but
evermore
joy

STEPHEN CRAMER's first book of poems, *Shiva's Drum*, was selected for the National Poetry Series and published by University of Illinois Press. *Bone Music*, his sixth, won the Louise Bogan Award. His ninth, *The Disintegration Loops*, was a finalist for the Vermont Book Award. He is also the editor of *Turn It Up! Music in Poetry from Jazz to Hip-Hop*. Cramer's work has appeared in journals such as *The American Poetry Review*, *African American Review*, *The Yale Review*, and *Harvard Review*. He teaches writing and literature at the University of Vermont and lives with his wife and teenager in Burlington.

Shanti Arts

Nature · Art · Spirit

Please visit us online
to browse our entire book catalog,
including poetry collections and fiction,
books on travel, nature, healing, art,
photography, and more.

Also take a look at our highly regarded art
and literary journal, *Still Point Arts Quarterly*,
which may be downloaded for free.

www.shantiarts.com

www.ingramcontent.com/pod-product-compliance
Lightning Source LLC
Chambersburg PA
CBHW042134160426